Wild Ones
Observing City Critters

By Carol L. Malnor

Illustrated by Cathy Morrision

Dawn Publications

For my dog-loving brother, Charles Lattimer — CLM

For my book-loving women artist friends in "Text in the City."
Thanks for the fun, inspiration, and friendship! — CM

Copyright © 2016 Carol L. Malnor
Illustrations copyright © 2016 Cathy Morrison

Special thanks to author Fran Hodgkins who provided the idea for this urban adventure in her book *Animals Among Us: Living with Suburban Animals*. Two very special dogs provided the inspiration for Scooter: Buddy, a rambunctious labradoodle (owner Janis Skeahan) and Tessa, a curious corgi (owner Barbara Gable). — CLM.

Library of Congress Cataloging-in-Publication Data
Malnor, Carol.
  Wild ones : critters in the city / by Carol L. Malnor ; illustrated by
Cathy Morrison. -- First edition.
      pages cm
  Summary: "Nature is all around us, even in the city. Follow Scooter, a rambunctious
dog, as he uses all of his senses to discover city critters, from ducks to falcons,
and skunks to coyotes. But he doesn't notice all of them. That's up to the reader.
'Explore More' endnotes provide information about city animals as well as activity
suggestions"-- Provided by the publisher.
  Includes bibliographical references.
  ISBN 978-1-58469-553-0 (hardback) -- ISBN 978-1-58469-554-7 (pbk.) 1.
Urban animals--Juvenile fiction. [1. Urban animals--Fiction. 2.
Dogs--Fiction.] I. Morrison, Cathy, illustrator. II. Title.
  PZ10.3.M2967Wi 2016
  [E]--dc23
                              2015017751

Book design and computer production by Patty Arnold, *Menagerie Design & Publishing*
Manufactured by Regent Publishing Services, Hong Kong

Printed December, 2015, in ShenZhen, Guangdong, China

10 9 8 7 6 5 4 3 2 1
First Edition

DAWN PUBLICATIONS
12402 Bitney Springs Road
Nevada City, CA 95959
530-274-7775
nature@dawnpub.com

Nature is all around us, even in the city. Follow Scooter as he uses his senses to discover city critters.

It's sunrise when Scooter sneaks out the back door.

He *doesn't see* the tracks in the mud or the sleeping raccoon. What he *does see* is a furry tail.

And the chase is on!

The squirrel scurries up a tree and scolds Scooter from a safe perch. Scooter ignores the squirrel and just keeps running.

He *doesn't notice* the mother opossum curled up with her babies underneath the shed. But he *does notice* a loud noise—
"quack, quack, quack."

Dashing around the corner, Scooter begins his city critter discoveries.

A mother mallard "quack, quack, quacks" to her ducklings. She's telling them it's time to leave their nest on the ledge. One by one they fearlessly jump. A passerby gives each one a soft landing.

Scooter *isn't aware* of the pigeon feathers floating through the air or the falcon flying away with a "bird breakfast" in its talons. But he soon *becomes aware* of an unfamiliar sound.

He scampers off to discover what it is.

Thwack! Thwack! A beaver slaps a warning
with its tail and slips under the water.

Scooter *doesn't know* there are hundreds of bats asleep under
the bridge. But he *does know* that
a gull carrying a bag is very strange.

He trots off to investigate.

The gull boldly marches down the sidewalk with its stolen prize—a bag of chips.

Scooter *doesn't spot* a rat as it scurries back to its hiding place. But he *does spot* a starling as it swoops low across the street.

Always curious about what he might discover, Scooter follows the bird.

Starlings are the darlings of fast food parking lots where they gobble up dropped French fries.

Scooter scrounges for something to eat, too. He *doesn't detect* the hairy legs of the giant spider that hitchhiked from South America in a banana box.

But after his snack, he *does detect* movement in a clump of weeds.

He wanders over to check it out.

Scooter is having such fun discovering city critters. But meanwhile, his family is worried.

Tap, tap, tap...they post signs.

Tap, tap, tap...a woodpecker replies.

Scooter

LOST!

The kids *completely miss* the huge swarm of ants crawling out of a crack in the sidewalk. But they *can't miss* the crows taking a puddle bath.

Scooter keenly *watches* a snake slithering
through the weeds of a vacant lot.

But, oh no!

He *should be watching* that dogcatcher.

Just in time, Scooter skedaddles into a
community garden.

He *doesn't catch* sight of a hungry rabbit, but he
does catch a whiff of a stinky smell.

Scooter decides not to hang around.

What luck! He finds a stick! Scooter
settles down to give it a good chew.

He *doesn't look* up to see the hawk's nest it fell
from until poop plops on his head. That darn
bird! So he *does look* for somewhere else to go.

Honk, honk! Flap, flap, flap!

Geese make a huge commotion as Scooter slips and slides through their slimy droppings. Eeew! Scooter *doesn't discover* the coyote lurking in the shadows. But he *does discover* a pile of something under an oak tree.

He sneaks over to investigate.

Underneath an owl's favorite roosting
spot, Scooter sniffs a pile of pellets—
the coughed up bones and fur of
the owl's prey.

He *doesn't hear* the fox kits quietly
"yip-yip-yipping." But when he *hears*
an owl loudly "hoo-hoo-hooing," Scooter
realizes it's almost dark.

And he makes a beeline for home.

Scooter *doesn't see* the bats
swooping through the sky
. . . or the opossum
walking across the
fence with babies on her back . . .
or the raccoons cooling off in
the wading pool.

But he *does see* his family. And that's
the very best discovery of all!

Scooter Shouldn't Scoot

Scooter had a big adventure in the city. But it's *never* good for dogs to run loose. Scooter was lucky he found his way home without getting hurt. Dogs in the city should *always* be on a leash or inside a fenced yard.

Getting Squirrelly

Squirrels are everywhere in the city. Did you see one on every page? What was it doing?

Sitting	Digging
Sleeping	Eating
Running	Jumping
Hiding	Climbing
Resting	Scolding
Scratching	Peeking

More to Find

Scooter saw a lot of wild animals as he traveled around the city. But there were some he *didn't* see. Find these critters in the illustrations.

Lady bird beetles are also called lady bugs. They eat insects that eat plants.

The red coloring on male **house finches** comes from the food they eat.

Moths are attracted to lights. Scientists don't know why. It's still a mystery.

Some **monarch butterflies** migrate 2000 miles or more every year.

Pigeons were brought to North America for food over 400 years ago.

Ruby-throated hummingbirds beat their wings so fast that they make a humming sound—about 300 beats a minute.

Bald eagles are not really bald. Their heads are covered with white feathers.

Male **fireflies** are also called lightning bugs. They flash their light to attract females.

Some **black bears** have stopped hibernating because they get food from garbage cans and dumpsters all year long.

Daily News
Bear Dumpster Dives for Food!

Eighteen **house sparrows** were brought to the US from England in 1851. Now they live in every state except Alaska.

A **toad's** eyes stick out. This allows it to see in all directions without moving its head.

American robins like to splash and drink water at birdbaths.

Feral cats are domesticated cats that have returned to living in the wild.

White-tailed deer are known for their fast running and high jumping. They're also great swimmers.

Is it *Really* True?

Did a man catch ducklings jumping off a ledge?

Yes! Mallard ducks usually nest on the ground. But one mallard mama made her nest on the ledge of a building. When the baby ducklings hatched, they needed to get down to the ground. The first duckling jumped and landed with a thud. A man working in the building saw what happened. He ran outside and caught the other ducklings. Then he carried them to a nearby river as their mama waddled behind.

Do beavers cut down city trees?

Yes! Some of the famous cherry trees in Washington, D.C., were cut down by a family of beavers. Beavers need to be close to water and are most active at night. One beaver can cut down a tree that's 10-inches in diameter in about 6 minutes. To save the cherry trees, the beavers were carefully trapped and taken to a woods away from the city.

Can a gull carry a bag of chips?

Yes! Not only can they carry chips, one gull learned to shoplift them. Each day it would walk into a store and grab a bag of corn chips. The store owner wanted to shoo the gull away. But many people liked to watch the bold gull, so they paid the store's owner for the chips it stole.

Do hawks make nests made of sticks on tall buildings?

Yes! A red-tailed hawk in New York City has been making stick nests every year since 2002. People gather across the street in Central Park to watch him.

His name is Pale Male. He's so famous he has his own website.

Will raccoons sit in a kid's wading pool?

Yes! It happened at my house! I heard a commotion outside in the middle of the night. When I turned on the yard light, I saw two raccoons lounging in our little pool. It was a hot summer night in California, and they were cooling off.

How Animals Adapt to the City

Opossums secretly live close to houses. They often eat pet food that is left outside.

Bats that usually live in caves have adapted to living under bridges.

Rats have learned to eat human food and garbage. Many have lost their fear of humans.

Peregrine falcons eat other birds. City pigeons are an easy prey for them to catch.

Odorous ants have adapted well to the city. Their "super colonies" cover an underground area as big as an entire city block.

Garter snakes used to be more common in cities. But fewer vacant lots mean fewer snakes.

Just like Scooter, we often go about our day without really noticing all of the animals that live around us. We might see a few, but miss many, many others. Scooter's adventure encourages children to increase their awareness of their animal neighbors.

Where is Home Sweet Home?

Scooter's city is an imaginary city, but the animals he sees (or doesn't see) are common throughout most of the U.S. Some scenes and situations in the story are based on incidents in specific cities. For example: The duckling incident happened in Spokane, Washington; bald eagles live on an island in the Potomac River in Washington, DC; a huge bat colony roosts under a bridge in Austin, Texas; and red-tailed hawks nest in New York City.

You may think that deer, foxes, and coyotes are too wild to live in cities. However, these animals are becoming very common in many city neighborhoods and suburbs, and they're moving closer to the center of metropolitan areas. They've been spotted in the busiest U.S. cities—Chicago, Los Angeles, and New York City.

Meeting Basic Needs

In order to survive, all living things need to live in a place where they can meet their basic needs of food, water, air, and a habitat with the right temperature.

Some animals have been city-dwellers for many, many years, such as pigeons, rats, and squirrels. Other animals have more recently moved to the city from wilder areas, including rabbits, falcons, bats, coyotes, eagles, beavers, gulls, geese, foxes, and deer. They may have come because their habitat has diminished or because they've discovered ways to find food and shelter in a city environment. Still other animals, such as bear, cougars, and moose are strictly "tourists"— they wander into a city looking for food, but don't live there.

Activity: Observation — Have children choose an animal to watch in their neighborhood. Ask them observe it for several days to discover how its needs are met. These questions will help with their observations: What time did you see the animal? What is the color and shape of its eyes, ears, nose, mouth or beak, and feet. What is the color and pattern of fur, feathers, skin, or shell? What does it eat? How does it move? What kinds of tracks does it leave? Where does it get water? Scan the QR Code for more observation questions and to read "Tips For Seeing More Animals."

Love 'Em or Hate 'Em

Wildlife in the city can be a complicated and controversial matter. Just about every animal found in the city has its fans and detractors.

Non-native species are particularly unappreciated. Pigeons, starlings, and house sparrows were brought into the U.S. from Europe and intentionally released. They compete with native species for food and habitat.

This story for young children does not include aspects of human attempts at animal control. However, if children have heard about such things as shooting coyotes, removing bears, or trapping foxes, it may be good to remind them that there are no "good" or "bad" animals. All animals are just living their lives the best they can. Learning about the animals that live in your area is the first step in wise decision-making about how to live with them.

Please remind children not to interfere with the normal activities of city critters. People should never touch wildlife, even if the animal seems friendly.

How Birds Adapt

"Birds are by far the most common vertebrate wildlife we see in the places we live, whether we are urban, suburban, or rural dwellers," says Lyanda Lynn Haupt, in *The Urban Bestiary*. "Birds are not just the most numerous wild things among us, but also the most lively and most easily observable." Many birds have adapted well to urban living:

- Crows like to roost in cities during the winter because it's warmer and there are fewer predators.

- In the wild, woodpeckers "drum" on trees to announce "this is my territory." In cities, they "drum" on telephone poles.

- Skyscrapers provide good nesting areas for peregrine falcons. Plus there are fewer falcon predators in the city.

- The short grass and small ponds found in public parks and golf courses make an ideal habitat for Canada geese. With plenty of food and few predators, some Canada geese have stopped migrating and have become year-round residents in cities.

Activity: *Identification* — Identifying birds can feel overwhelming. Haupt suggests beginning with the five most common birds that live around your house (or school yard), such as house sparrows, robins, crows, house finches, and starlings. Learn everything you can about each bird. Then, when you're ready, add five more. "BirdSleuth K-12," a program through Cornell Lab of Ornithology, provides free educational materials. http://www.birdsleuth.org/

How Mammals Adapt

Of all the mammals found in cities, raccoons, squirrels, and rats have adapted most easily to the urban environment. They're so common that many people don't think of them as wildlife. Just like birds mammals have discovered how to adapt to city living.

- Rabbits find just the right habitat in city gardens. Although usually nocturnal, naturalists have observed that city rabbits are more active in the daytime, possibly because there is plenty of food and few predators.

- Foxes are highly adaptable omnivores. A city culvert makes a good den to hide fox kits.

- Skunks, born and raised in city habitats, often show no fear of humans.

- Deer live in fringe areas, such as parks and golf courses. Their populations in suburbs are exploding because of abundant food and few predators.

- Rats are among the many animals that have learned to thrive on human food and garbage.

Resources

- Cornell Lab of Ornithology has several projects, including Celebrate Urban Birds, Project FeederWatch, and BirdSleuth K-12.

- National Wildlife Federation also has several programs: Create a Certified Wildlife Habitat, Wildlife Watch, and Garden for Wildlife.

- The Urban Wildlife Institute, a research center at Chicago's Lincoln Park Zoo, studies the ecology of urban animals. Its Chicago Wildlife Watch citizen science project, www.chicagowildlifewatch.org, lets anyone around the world participate in urban animal research while they learn to identify city animals.

- *What the Robin Knows: How Birds Reveal the Secrets of the Natural World* by Jon Young, Mariner Books (2013)

- *The Urban Bestiary: Encountering the Everyday Wild* by Lyanda Lynn Haupt, Little, Brown and Co. (2013)

Use the QR Code to go to an Activities page where you may access educational resources and standards-based lesson plans. You'll also find downloads for "Tips to See More Animals" and "How to Be a Good Neighbor to Wildlife" and links to Youtube videos of city critters, including bats flying out from a bridge in Texas, a man catching ducklings in Washington, foxes hiding in a city culvert, and Pale Male nesting in NYC.

About the Author

Carol Malnor grew up in a suburb of Chicago where an urban park looked like the vast wilderness to her young eyes. She fondly remembers chasing after the family beagle that scooted down the alley whenever the back gate was left ajar. Now living in northern California with her husband, Bruce, she delights in the critters she sees on her daily walk—squirrels, raccoons, deer, birds of all sizes, and the occasional raccoon in her backyard! As a teacher for over 25 years, Carol regularly incorporated nature studies into her classroom. This is Carol's seventh book for Dawn.

Other Books by Carol L. Malnor

On Kiki's Reef — A tiny baby sea turtle scrambles across the sandy beach and into the sea. Floating far out in the ocean, Kiki becomes a gentle giant and meets a fascinating community of creatures on a coral reef.

Molly's Organic Farm is based on the true story of a homeless cat that found herself in the wondrous world of an organic farm. Seen through Molly's eyes, we discover the interplay of nature that grows wholesome food.

The BLUES Go Birding (co-authored with Sandy Fuller) — Three books that introduce the fascinating world of birds to children. The information is accurate and useful for a young birder, and presented with a generous helping of humor:

> *The BLUES Go Birding Across America*
> *The BLUES Go Birding At Wild America's Shores*
> *The BLUES Go Extreme Birding*

The Earth Heroes Series — Each of these books for middle school children presents the biographies of eight of the world's greatest naturalists, with special attention not only to their careers and lasting contributions, but also to events in their youth that foreshadowed greatness:

> *Earth Heroes: Champions of the Wilderness*
> *Earth Heroes: Champions of Wild Animals*

Nature Portals Card Deck — The 52 cards in this deck combine nature photos with uplifting words to expand your awareness of nature's gifts. Take the cards with you on a nature outing; or when you're unable to get outside, look at the photos to feel immersed in the natural world.

About the Illustrator

Cathy Morrison is an award-winning illustrator who lives in Colorado, within view of both the Great Plains and the Rocky Mountains. She watches the plants, the animals, and rain—all close up and personal. She began her career in animation and graphic design, but discovered her passion for children's book illustration while raising her two children. After several years illustrating with traditional media, she now works digitally, which helps the publisher adapt the art into interactive book apps. This is Cathy's fifth book for Dawn Publications.

Some Other Books from Dawn Publications

Noisy Bird Sing-Along invites readers to make some noise! Every kind of bird has its very own kind of sound —from cheerful to mournful and from sweet to weird. Find out what birds are in your neighborhood without even opening your eyes. Also:

> *Noisy Bug Sing-Along*
> *Noisy Frog Sing-Along*

Lifetimes — Beginning with the lifetime of a mayfly (one day) and concluding with the age of the universe (about 15 to 20 billion years) readers are introduced to some of nature's longest, shortest, and most unusual lifetimes. The overall message is "All life is important on our planet Earth."

The Dandelion Seeds's Big Dream — This charming tale follows the flight of a seed from the countryside into the city where it is buffeted by wind, caught in a spider web, and trapped in trash. Readers will be surprised and delighted to find out where the tiny seed finally lands.

The Prairie that Nature Built — A wild prairie is a lively place in this rhythmic romp. You'll learn about the plants and critters that depend upon one of the most endangered ecological systems in the world.

Dawn Publications is dedicated to inspiring in children a deeper understanding and appreciation for all life on Earth. You can browse through our titles, download resources for teachers, and order at www.dawnpub.com or call 800-545-7475.